MEDAL DAY *at the*

M^(AC)DOWELL COLONY

1960-1993

MEDAL DAY AT THE MACDOWELL COLONY

Copyright ©1994 by the MacDowell Colony, Inc., all rights reserved. No part of this book may be reproduced or transmitted in any form or by any means, electronic or mechanical, including photocopying, recording, or by any information storage or retrieval system, without the written permission of the copyright holder.

ISBN 0-942389-08-5
Manufactured in the United States

ACKNOWLEDGMENTS

THE COLONY is indebted to Excelsior Printing Company, North Adams, Massachusetts; Corey McPherson Nash, Watertown, Massachusetts, for the design; Shearman & Sterling and, in particular, its associate Michael Bonarti, for their advice and counsel; Nancy Hayes Clune, for copy-editing; and to Sherri Monson for her preparation of the manuscript. We wish to thank Alfred A. Knopf, Inc., for its permission to print the excerpt from John Hersey's speech.

There is a shortage in this world of people to whom the arts are not merely an ornament but a force of life as necessary as food and air and love.

RUSSELL LYNES ON
EUDORA WELTY
1970

PREFACE

THIS VOLUME includes a limited selection of excerpts from speeches made on Medal Day at the MacDowell Colony in Peterborough, New Hampshire. Some passages are taken from introductory remarks, and others are from acceptance speeches made by the Medalists. The purpose of the book is to illustrate the unique perspective that a variety of composers, visual artists, writers, and critics bring to the creative process rather than to record all of the speeches made over the past years.

The Edward MacDowell Medal recognizes extraordinary creativity. Since 1960, thirty-three Edward MacDowell Medals have been awarded to painters, sculptors, writers, composers, photographers, and filmmakers, chosen by their peers as persons whose work has made an exceptional contribution to our culture. The MacDowell Colony, founded in 1907 by Edward and Marian MacDowell, exists to give artists of professional stature an opportunity to work under highly favorable conditions. The Colony's character grew out of the experience of Edward MacDowell, who found that both the quality and amount of his music were improved by the opportunity to work in a secluded cabin on his farm. Today's Colony operates on the pattern that developed out of MacDowell's needs as a working artist and from his conviction that the companionship of artists from different disciplines enriched his life and his work.

This book was made possible by the generosity of Lyell C. Dawes of Cobblestone Publishing, who has published it for the Colony. He has had a firm hand in guiding its form and content.

MARY CARSWELL
EXECUTIVE DIRECTOR
THE MACDOWELL COLONY

INTRODUCTION

I READ A FEW pages of this book and had to stop to make a note, thinking, "I must remember that." I went on reading, stopped again and, when I had finished the book, had six pages of observations so apt or useful I couldn't let them slip away.

This is a book of gems, not surprising because it celebrates, as William Styron says, "the brightest constellation of American talent that could be assembled in the latter half of this century." The words remembered here are those measured out by colleagues and critics to explain individual stars in that constellation of MacDowell Medal winners.

They capture essences: of late August afternoons under a tent in New Hampshire; of the simplicity and modesty of great talent; of the sweat it takes to describe genius. Dore Ashton, talking of Willem de Kooning, asks, "What do we do with our contemporaries? We cancel them with hyperbole."

There is no hyperbole here, but informed and conscientious homage, due reverence to men and women who will outlive hyperbole.

It is, in every way I can think of, appropriate that these celebrations take place at the MacDowell Colony, a place where such judgments are made every day by creative people struggling to be honest with themselves, beyond the din and distortions of the marketplace, where hyperbole reigns. So this careful award celebrates the spirit of the Colony itself.

When Leonard Bernstein was the medalist in 1987, Ned Rorem said, "Successful people, if they have brains, don't think of themselves as successful. They know what the public does not know: they know what they've not yet done."

The delicious thing about the MacDowell Colony is that, every day of the year, it is full of people—successful or not—who know what they've not yet done. The energy of that knowledge is loud in the forest silence of the Colony and it is a lovely sound.

>   ROBERT MACNEIL
>   CHAIRMAN
>   THE MACDOWELL COLONY

I came here when I had had nothing published at all, except in undergraduate publications, but their kindness had found me out; and, oh how I needed it, needed to hear myself think and to get out of all this tumult with which I both was deeply engaged and not unhappy in, but in which there was no chance, really, to explore oneself. And then it went on for quite a while, because it was some time before I was able to find any other way—to find this inner concentration.

THORNTON WILDER
1960

MEDAL DAY *at the*

M<small>AC</small>DOWELL COLONY

1960-1993

VISUAL

IT'S THE FIRST TIME

THAT REALLY INVITES

A NEW SOLUTION;

ARTISTS

I MEAN, HAVING DONE IT ONCE,

THERE'S NO POINT

IN DOING IT TWICE.

THEREFORE, I NEVER

DO TWO THINGS ALIKE.

ISAMU NOGUCHI
1982

MEYER SHAPIRO *on* ALEXANDER CALDER
1963

Calder is not only an extraordinary artist by virtue of the quality of his work as sculpture; he is also an inventor. His mobiles are a new kind of object that gives an immediate delight. Few artists who create a style of their own also invent, as he has done, a new field of art. He has added to sculpture surprising forms that change our conception of what this art can be. For one who comes to Calder's work with only the old examples of sculpture in mind, it will seem a complete denial of the art; no modeling, no compact block, no rich light and shade, no pedestal, no precious or noble materials and complex techniques, no trace of the sculptor's hand in subtleties of finish. And in the expression, none of the pathos, striving, heroism or symbolized ideals that have been expected of sculpture since ancient times. His work appears rather as the amusement of a whimsical mechanic playing with the everyday techniques of the metal shop and factory. While the layman, before a Mondrian or a Pollock, says: "My child can do it" (unfortunately, the children have not obliged us and we must still depend on the artists), before a Calder mobile the handy American who repairs his own car says: "I can do it myself." Like Brunelleschi's egg, it looks easy once you have seen it done. The public has expressed its feeling for the simplicity and naturalness of this art in accepting it so readily as a part of its own world. It evokes directly the fascination of forms in movement, latent in all of us, whereas the visual in art is most often overlaid by symbols and ideas that make us think and remember instead of see.

If Calder has created a type of construction that satisfies a common taste—a model that even incites the layman to spontaneous imitation—he has produced an immense number of variations on it—a sign of the true inventor who is thoroughly at home with his invention. He is a fortunate artist who found a vein that he has been able to exploit freely for a lifetime without exhaustion and without being distracted by the discoveries of others. He has carried on with strength, with grace and humor, and with an exacting attention to quality. What he does is well-rooted in his own being and is in such harmony with his surroundings that he has enjoyed in the esoteric art of sculpture a popular success rarely won by an original artist in our time. His work takes its place in modern buildings with an air of predestined fitness, as the old massive figures in the stone architecture of the past.

Behind his seemingly innocent juggling with bits of metal is the powerful trend of modern art since the 1860s. While his work looks peculiarly American in the fresh use of industrial

Like Brunelleschi's egg,
it looks easy once you have seen it done.

techniques, it depends on the release of imagination in sculpture that came about through the revolutionary work of a line of great painters and sculptors in Europe several decades before him. Calder has lived at the top of the world art of his time. No inspired mechanic transporting to the studio the tools, materials and methods of the factory could have achieved this result. Only a sculptor who had absorbed the most advanced European art of the first quarter of our century, with its radical inventiveness, could have produced such a work. It presupposes the disengagement of lines, points and surfaces as freely disposable elements of operation, unconstrained by requirements of likeness, and the discovery of the beauty of smooth planes, open forms, transparencies, pivoted and suspended wholes. It may be that the particular combination of the mechanical and the artistic—so often regarded as antagonists—was first possible only for an American and one with Calder's special experience and temperament. But though his art suggests the stimulus of the machine, there is little of the familiar ideology of machine aesthetics in his elegant and fanciful constructions. It seems to me that they have a more interesting and significant affinity with nature, with trees, flowers and sensitive marine organisms, like the sea anemone, with whatever responds delicately to wind and water and is balanced on a slender flexible support. The sustained appeal of his work, the joy it arouses, are akin to our feeling before the suspended or floating existence in organic nature, yielding lightly to the forces of the surroundings, while retaining its own forms in ever-changing positions. His works touch, I believe, old and deep responses to passive movement and lability in ourselves. Seen from this point of view Calder's art is of a high and poetic order of sculptural imagination. It unites in vision, as only art can do by its perfected forms, qualities of the world about us with our own natures.

JOHN CANADAY on LOUISE NEVELSON 1969

After Louise Nevelson had made good, a friend said to her once, "Well, Louise, what would have happened if it had turned out that you weren't good enough?" and Louise Nevelson said, in her matter-of-fact way, "Well, you know it never had occurred to me to be anything but first-rate." Now this has nothing to do with arrogance. It has everything to do with being an artist; because if you are not convinced you are going to be first-rate, the whole game isn't worth the candle.

When I say that Louise Nevelson's sculpture is, for me, an affirmation of faith, you can put it that she has taken much of the detritus of our civilization and has not simply recombined it; she has completely transformed it. You may recognize a balustrade, you may recognize a moulding, a dowel, planks of wood, etc.; but they are so transformed that their original function is simply no longer there. They are forms. They are forms transformed from detritus into what I would call a spiritual expression.

Almost every day we are subject to a thousand, a million, any number of stimuli. What we see, what we hear, what we read, what our experiences are, everything comes in to us. We absorb these experiences according to our capacity. A few of us not only absorb them but understand, assimilate, refine and distill from all this mass its essence. These are the understanding people.

Then there are a very few special people who have the capacity to create, to bring together all they have assimilated and produce from it a play, a poem, a sculpture, a painting. They tell us more about what we are doing and what we are all about than we ever realize until we see their expression of it.

DORE ASHTON on WILLEM DE KOONING 1975

Willem de Kooning lives among us, is our contemporary, and yet, in our flagrantly historicizing century, he is also remote from us. History has seized and plundered him. For more than fifty years he has followed the vocation of painter, and more than forty of those years were exclusively, obsessively given to painting. But what do we do with our contemporaries? We cancel them with hyperbole. Good bureaucrats, we register their classification, their rank, pin on a medal and look elsewhere.

By handing over our distinguished contemporaries as hostages to history, we flee the responsibility of close attention. De Kooning's work is quick and not dead; it is vigorously transpiring in our very own living space. It must be seen in its actual detail and only then in its totality as an oeuvre occupying a designated space in what we call history....

De Kooning's own insights are in the realm of painting, and I can't emphasize too much how different painting man is from writing man. Painting has its reasons which reason knows not. There is an old film showing Matisse painting from the model. In slow motion, his hand hovers, shudders, makes curious passes at the canvas, and goes through an unbelievable number of ritualized gestures before the brush touches the canvas. Matisse himself was astonished to see that his hand traveled its own course, and he drew the obvious moral. A painter's prime experience occurs in the act of painting. The whole construct of his experience while working is different from that of other artists. If a painter conquers territory, it is by imperceptible leaps, sudden juxtapositions, and the unexpected materializing—literally—of a sufficiently complex fusion of perceptions, feelings and ideas. A painter knows that his brush has its own language. Yet, the only reason we call painting, very lamely indeed, a language—and it can only be metaphorically—is because it shows forth things language cannot circumscribe. This is the despair of critics. The jibes at the diction of art critics are well merited, for the language of art criticism is of course ultimately and forever inadequate. What the painter is showing forth—those conjunctions of feelings, articulated in the terms of shapes, colors and spaces—is simply not available to the word.

Still, if we speak of de Kooning, we must try to find some means to talk about a painting man's space, for spatializing imaginatively and creating light is what he does. He is not just concerned with how it looks but how it feels. De Kooning's space and light demand that we perceive how it feels to move through these created spaces, and how entities moving through such charged spaces are re-formed, deformed, metamorphosed. Forms in de Kooning's paintings give way to sensations, and sensations give way to forms in this antiphonal language he has established.

The unity in de Kooning's life's work springs from his confidence in the language of the painter. If he paints figures or non-figures, or if, when he completes a painting, there are recognizable motifs, he asks: What's the difference? "In reality, it's nothing but painting." And that is the secret conviction of painters: A painting is in fact nothing but painting. A painting is more real to a painter, as Delacroix remarked wonderingly in his journal, than any pretext on which a painting may be based. All the same, painters strive to decode their own language. De Kooning for instance reads Wittgenstein. But which Wittgenstein? Perhaps the Wittgenstein who wrote: "It is obvious that an imagined world, however different it may be from the real one, must have something—a form—in common with it."

These forms of de Kooning and their peculiar rhythms are homologues of something, as Wittgenstein might have said, which we can or might experience. Although Wittgenstein's supreme effort to bestow clarity attracts de Kooning, there is in him another side, the Dostoyevskian darkness of the underground man who demands the right to do what may not be in his own best interest. A painting man, as opposed to a thinking man like Wittgenstein, must preserve his inherent respect for the irrational.

In our compulsive heaping of hyperbole we have tried to pin down de Kooning; to make him a functionary of art history. There are those who said, well, he is just an extension of expressionism, either the German kind or, like Soutine, the French. And there are those who said de Kooning just extends the Cubist tradition, in his own way, of course. Yet a really close reading of de Kooning's work supports neither claim but shows only that he has created a grand metaphor for quickness as opposed to deadness using all the devices in the painter's repertory. When de Kooning chose, he used collage, overlaps, vertiginously speeding lines, vignettes, profusions of details and reductions of details. He even used leitmotifs such as those teeth and eyes half-hidden in paintings throughout his career....

For the shape, in de Kooning's case, is the thing. The man who likes, or rather, loves shapes always works by association. De Kooning often points out the significance of shape, not only in classical painters, but in popular draftsmen such as Al Capp. In "L'il Abner," he says, Mammy Yokum wears a shape. We only know it's a hat by association. Shapes persist in

> **I CAN'T EMPHASIZE TOO MUCH HOW DIFFERENT PAINTING MAN IS FROM WRITING MAN.**

de Kooning's works. Even when, in the 1950s, he made landscape-like closeups, with great fragments of light, there was neither up nor down, but always an echo of shaping—a topological continuity.

Yet I say his work is metaphorical. It is not only about forms in space. Many have noticed the cursive aspect of de Kooning's line. His line does literally course. It is a line, as was Rembrandt's, that goes beyond description; a hooking, leaping line that vivifies space; a handwritten line tying up those nouns (or forms) into the language of painting. This looping line is always seeking and sensing locations of *somethings* in spaces. It is a line which can be used as Picasso did to repeat recognizable cues in unlikely places—as symbol in fact. But it can also be used to invoke specifically such nouns as haunch, belly, breast, eyes, teeth—all functions of de Kooning's line. Yet what his line writes is only to be known through all the other means he uses, above all through his meridional palette which, with its yellows, pinks, reds and sky blues, lets there be light....

In de Kooning's effort to know, really know, his images, drawing with his eyes closed is tantamount to an invocation to the gods. It is at once a gesture reflecting great doubt, and a gesture reflecting the same invincible conviction that kept Cézanne going. As de Kooning told David Sylvester: "You've developed a little culture for yourself, like yogurt; as long as you keep something of the original microbes, the original thing will grow out."

We recognize the original thing in de Kooning's culture as a full emotional response to existence, and as an embodiment of the deeper structures that underlie our lifelong gesturing.

JOHN CANADAY on RICHARD DIEBENKORN 1978

For some time now I've been calling Richard Diebenkorn the best American painter at work today. I don't like that term "best," but every time I give a talk somewhere and have questions from the audience, somebody asks me who is the best American painter at work today. There are too many ways of being good for there to be only one answer to that. I used to say Saul Steinberg, but Steinberg is too special a case and not really a painter, so lately I've settled on Richard Diebenkorn as coming closest to all-inclusive best painter. I should be able to talk about him rather easily, but now I discover that I can't explain Richard Diebenkorn very well and that everything I think of to say about him sounds either presumptuous or redundant.

So I am going to approach this by the back door—I'll get around to tying it up later—by saying that I think that American art would have been much better off the past twenty-five years if there had been no art critics, none at all. Art critics have abused their function, which is strictly and simply to evaluate works of art, which involves explaining them somewhat. But by evaluate I do not mean appraise. Criticism should not be a consumer's guide, which it has tended to become, nor should the critic be an art broker, which he has tended to become, especially when he is asked downright to give a recommendation for the purchase of a painting that is likely to increase in value. A critic should not affiliate himself with a clique of artists, dealers or museum curators. I hold that he really shouldn't even know artists, at least not while he's practicing criticism. I get a lot of fun out of knowing them now that I'm sort of retired, having reached the age of official senility about a year ago.

I think that the job of the critic is not to stimulate interest in art, not really. Above all it is not to stimulate interest in new movements just because they are new. The job is simply to watch developments and carry on as you go. Two critics whom I enjoyed and respected—Thomas Hess and Harold Rosenberg, both of whom died so tragically last month— couldn't agree with me less. I was in a debate with Thomas Hess once over national television, unfortunately, because he came out better than I did, and he said, "What do you stand for anyway? What are you for?" I had been fussing at him because he was so rabid about abstract expressionism that he couldn't talk about anything else at that time. That was fifteen or sixteen years ago. I said, "Well, I don't know, I guess I'm for good art," and he said, "Oh, come on now, anybody can be for good art. You can't just sit around waiting for things to happen, you've got to make something happen."

Well, I think that is absolutely the most absurd, outrageous and perverse possible approach to the practice of art criticism. Art should just happen. It always has happened and if you try to direct it, you are likely to put it off course. You are also likely to stimulate it the way overfeeding does a plant, producing a lot of unhealthy foliage for a little while but no roots. The idea that art should be stimulated in this way, the idea that new movements should be invented, is topsy-turvy. The critic-as-prophet or innovator of art movements is assuming that you can turn out an art which will produce a culture. Well, you can't. The culture produces the art and that's all there is to it. If the art doesn't come out of the culture and come naturally— I say "naturally" with many birth pangs perhaps on the part of the artist—then it isn't the real thing, it just isn't. The artist should lead, we should follow. Alfred Barr used to insist on that all the time at the Museum of Modern Art, and he really believed that the artists were leading and the museum was following, but I think really that what was happening then has been happening all along, which is not that the artists lead, but

THE CULTURE PRODUCES THE ART AND THAT'S ALL THERE IS TO IT.

that the artist's function as innovator has been taken over by a combine of artists, galleries, critics and museums.

I want to quote from Harold Rosenberg, a man like Tom Hess whose company I enjoyed although we had almost nothing in common as critics. The truth is the first time I met Harold Rosenberg was at a perfectly respectable dinner party, where I told him that if he wasn't so much bigger than I am I'd punch him in the nose. We've been friends ever since because he liked that, and he was so much bigger that I never had to carry out my bluff.

Harold Rosenberg wrote once that "The texture of collaboration between dealers, collectors, and exhibitors has become increasingly dense to the point where the artist is confronted by a solid wall of opinion and fashion forecasts constructed essentially out of the data of the art market." There's only one thing wrong with that: he left out a word. He left out the word "critics." He should have said, "The texture of collaboration between dealers, collectors, exhibitors, and critics has become increasingly dense to the point where the artist is confronted by a solid wall of opinion and fashion forecasts constructed essentially out of the data of the art market." He wrote that at a time when he was unhappy about developments away from his field of abstract expressionism. Apparently he didn't realize that he had been part of, that all us critics had been a part of—those of us who were effective, those of them who were effective, playing it very modestly—

that he had been an extremely influential part of that collaboration with dealers, collectors and exhibitors.

The result of this idea of inventing new movements, of deciding what should come next, of speeding up the whole development, has been a succession of refinements and counter movements beginning with abstract expressionism in the late 1950s. Early in the 1960s, Alfred Barr said, "I see a return to more hard edge abstraction and a revival of figure painting." That was quoted to his embarrassment in the magazine *Esquire*, I think. Barr had always avoided making prophecies, but both of these came true, although not in ways he expected. There was a revival of hard edge abstraction in the non-art movement called op art, which flourished briefly when the Museum of Modern Art announced that it was going to hold an exhibition of op art called "The Responsive Eye." There were op artists everywhere, as soon as that was announced, but op died quickly except for a few legitimate practitioners like Bridget Riley and Richard Anuszkiewicz. The revival of figure painting came in a way that seemed to puzzle and offend the Museum of Modern Art. This of course was pop art. (I missed the boat as a critic on pop art; I should have been right in there booming along for it, but I didn't realize how important and how good the best of it was until all the excitement was over and it was said to be passé.) Pop's vulgarity—a vital vulgarity—made it offensive to the Museum of Modern Art; also it was terribly American, and the Museum of Modern Art at that time was European-oriented. Abstract expressionism, for instance, was essentially the final expression of a European movement rather than an American one, in spite of the fact that it reached full flower in New York. It was a geographical difference only.

After pop art we had, not necessarily in this order, colorfield painting, minimal art, conceptual art, hyperrealism, photorealism, and somewhere in there in the lost and found department but never claimed by anybody as its own was something called cybernetic art, along with a lot of others. The progression was reasonable enough in many ways, especially in the direction of pure abstraction, on the principle of "less is more." If less is more, then less and less is bound to be more and more, less and less and less, more and more and more, until finally you get to the point where zero is totality. There may be some philosophical basis for that, I dare say in some mystical Indian religion, but I don't really think it works very well in art. You get minimal art and then from minimal you get conceptual where you don't even have to do anything. The textbooks now use as an example of conceptual art a piece of paper, I've forgotten by whom, on which is typed, "What I was not thinking about at 5:00 PM last Thursday night," or something like that, which gets pretty silly.

I realize that I'm reducing to absurdity many of these things to which I object, specifically minimal and conceptual art. Why were they so popular with some critics? The trouble with minimal art is precisely that it's minimal, but having no content of its own it offered maximum verbal range to the critics. You can write indefinitely about minimal art and never reach the end of it because there is nothing in the world in minimal art to contradict anything in the world you say.

I think maybe it's time for me to take my bearings in this talk. I said I was coming in by the back door—so what does all of this have to do with Richard Diebenkorn? Just this: Richard Diebenkorn has been an artist free from this voguishness. Free from following. If he ever faced that "solid wall of fashion forecast," he paid no attention to it. When abstract expressionism was on the rise, he was a first-rate abstract expressionist, but when

> *He has not been one of those overfertilized talents with a lot of blossoms and no roots, soon dying.*

abstract expressionism became the rage, Richard Diebenkorn didn't capitalize on his position. My impression from standing on the outside looking in is that abstract expressionism had given Richard Diebenkorn what it had to give him by the time it reached its greatest vogue. Diebenkorn was one of the first artists of any reputation to, I don't want to say revert, that's not right, to figurative painting, but to progress to another phase of figurative painting. Then when figurative painting came back strong, we have Richard Diebenkorn deciding that he has learned what that had to give him, and going into the period of abstraction which he is now following, when abstraction is supposed to be on the same wane.

Richard Diebenkorn has been wonderful proof that an artist does not have to follow the fashion, and, above all, that he may seem to go back to passé movements while all the time he is progressing forward to something personal, something new that he has to give. His art has matured; he has not been one of those overfertilized talents with a lot of blossoms and no roots, soon dying. His art has matured because he has remained outside the arena.

JOHN SZARKOWSKI *on* LEE FRIEDLANDER 1986

Photography is surely the easiest of the arts—unless perhaps it is more difficult than lyric poetry, which requires only that a few ordinary words, the common property of us all, be put in the right order. But in honor of this occasion let us agree that photography is the easiest. Putting aside for today the not very mysterious mysteries of craft, a photographer finally does nothing but stand in the right place, at the right time, and decide what should fall within and what outside the rectangle of the frame. That is what it comes down to.

Complications can of course be devised, and are continually devised, to provide hiding places from the awful simplicity of the problem, but they do not hide enough, and they do not last. The transparency of photography is the curse under which the serious photographer lives, for it reveals with cruel impartiality whether he or she was on a given day alert or distracted, singular or conventional, open to the infinite possibilities of the world or a captive of past successes.

It is not surprising then that many, even among the very greatest of photographers, have done their original work within the span of a decade and then have repeated themselves, or have retreated to less exposed positions as teachers or journalists or curators, where failure of concentration and the atrophy of sensibility are less likely to be noticed. A decade of original work is of course a miracle, and it would be vulgar even to wonder whether Keats or Schubert would have given us more. Still, our hunger for evidence of the possibility of renewal makes us cherish especially the long creative lives—the examples of Titian, and Matisse, and Dr. Johnson.

In photography there is Eugene Atget, who began in middle age and who, until his death thirty-five years later, got better and better. Three times Alfred Steiglitz came to the end of a line of thought and then, after a pause, began again with a new thought. Edward Weston's work became progressively complex and humane until his work was finally slowed by illness.

From Lee Friedlander we have had, so far, a quarter-century of surprise and nourishment. His work of the sixties is surely one of the lasting triumphs of the historic sensibility that was called puns, sotto voce jokes and high-wire gamesmanship. The mood of the work then was one of good-tempered ironic detachment. However marginal the real value of the real world, it was a perfect place to make photographs, the wit and quality of which redeemed their subject matter and transferred trivialities into fables. That earlier Friedlander was a superb flâneur who loved the boulevards for the materials they supplied his art. I am aware of no sudden changes in Friedlander's work. He works every day, like a shoemaker or a priest, and one day's work seems much like that of the previous day. In a year, the work has changed a little. Each seven years, approximately the length of time it takes for us to replace all of the cells in our bodies, we have had a new Friedlander, as though he were not simply an artist but a natural principle.

Some fifteen years after Friedlander's first public successes, and in time for this country's bicentennial celebration, he produced a book of 213 photographs describing his choice from the marvelously various and touching congregation of celebratory monuments that fill our country: tributes to the volunteer fire department, to the pioneers, to Tom Mix's horse, Trigger, to liberty, to motherhood, to the founding fathers of every state and township, and, of course, to the dead warriors—one hundred thousand monuments to how many dead warriors. This great book contains pictures made over a period of perhaps a dozen years. The latter of those had moved away from irony, away from found cubism, from visual sleight of hand,

and had shifted to a style that seemed in comparison almost an uninflected naturalism, to the description of facts that Friedlander found important and beautiful.

Perhaps the most surprising quality of *The American Monument* was the deep sympathy of it. We are, of course, impressed by the easy grace of the pictures. They recall the work of a superior juggler who arranges his plates and oranges so equitably in their parabola that they seem scarcely to move. But I think we are moved more deeply by Friedlander's intuitions concerning the nature of America's relationship to its past, concerning the vernacular materials out of which with attention we might fashion a culture, concerning the evidence of these countless attempts to preserve and nourish the idea of community. I am still astonished and heartened by the deep affection in those pictures, by the photographer's tolerant equanimity in the face of the facts, by the generosity of spirit, the freedom from pomposity and rhetoric. One might call this work an act of high artistic patriotism, an achievement that might help us reclaim that word from ideologues and expediters.

More broadly still, there is in Friedlander's mature work, it seems to me, a disinterested rigor, a clear-eyed, unsentimental respect for those potentials of the world and those potentials of his art that would exist in his absence. In this sense his art is, without servility to received opinions, a social art.

His work, in sum, constitutes a conversation among the symbols that we live among and that to some degree we live by. It reminds us of the strength of an alternative American tradition to that of Thoreau and Whitman and Steiglitz, with its constant insistence on the big I. His work recalls Thomas Eakins, the painter; and Walker Evans, the photographer; and Wallace Stevens, who said, "It is important to believe that the visible is the equivalent of the invisible. And once we believe it, we have destroyed the imagination. That is to say, we have destroyed the false imagination." And William Carlos Williams, who said, "No ideas, but in things."

LEE FRIEDLANDER
1986

When they sent me the list of the Medal winners before, I was very taken aback to be in that crowd, and I thought of something that happened to me fifteen years ago or so. I was walking through a state fair—I think all photographers love parades and fairs; I certainly do. I was walking through a home economics building, and there was quite a large wall, as long as this tent, full of the most beautiful quilts. I was looking at them quite carefully because they were very touching. I got to the one that won the blue ribbon, and I stood there awestruck. All the hair on my body went on end. It was a quilt made by a lady who had made it out of all the ribbons—red, blue and white—that she had won in her life, and it was the size of a double bed. It was not only beautiful, but it was her history, and it showed such care and sweet labor. I just hope that we artists come up to that condition.

John Szarkowski wrote opposite one of my photographs once—in a book called *Looking at Photographs*, "The point of the game is to know love and serve sight, and the basic strategic problem is to find the new kind of clarity within the prickly thickets of unordered sensation." Well, I immediately went out and started photographing prickly thickets. Sometimes clothed in cherries. But I think it's true.

Being the first photographer [to get the Medal], I thought that I should probably explain what photography was, but the more I thought about it, the less I was able to. I did read something; maybe some of you will understand, maybe you won't, I don't know. It was a book called *Water Music* by T. Coraghessan Boyle, an adventure story taking place in Africa. The hero, a British explorer, is lost in the bowels of

Northern Africa, and his party and guides have either been abandoned or killed. Since he has no supplies and no money (it's all been robbed), he finds his only asset is that they recognize him as an educated man because he can write. So he gets his meals, as he's trying to meander toward where he thinks he will be salvaged or get back to England, by writing little notes for people.

One day a rich merchant has had him in and has given him a very fine lunch. In return, he asks him to write in chalk on a large blackboard a particular message from the Koran. Our hero very carefully writes on the blackboard the Lord's Prayer. When the writing is finished, the merchant smiles very happily, takes a wet towel, washes the board clean, then wrings the towel into a glass and drinks the contents, with gusto and happiness. Isn't that like photography?

> *We're a restless kind of hunters....*
> *We're always on the prowl,*
> *not knowing sometimes*
> *what we are after,*
> *but we are out there.*

That's about photography. Now about photographers. We're a restless kind of hunters. We have to go places somehow to make pictures; you can't make a picture of Los Angeles from Boston. So we're always on the prowl, not knowing sometimes what we are after, but we are out there. The best description I have heard of that, to describe such a creature, is by the great blues singer Joe Turner, who sings a wonderful song called "Shake, Rattle and Roll." In it, there's a line that goes "like a one-eyed cat peepin' in a seafood store."

ELODIE OSBORN on STAN BRAKHAGE 1989

Setting frame by frame on moving film involves the same process as putting paint on canvas, placing notes on a musical staff, or writing one word after another. Moreover, many artists had turned from painting and sculpture to film in order to explore the perception of movement. The sensation of the resulting flow of images is an aesthetic experience particular to our time. But the choice of images must be made by artists in whatever medium from their thoughts, feelings and sensitivity to the life around them or within them.

One of the reasons we chose to honor Stan Brakhage is because he, perhaps longer than any other independent filmmaker in America, has made films, starting as a teenager, purely out of his own personal visions. In fact he has stated that he finds an antagonism between language and vision and needs to render thoughts and feeling in visual terms alone.

Americans seem to have a great deal of trouble understanding the work of visual artists. For some reason a statement made in visual terms often comes under attack, especially of late, by those in political power. One wonders why. Is it because we are such a young culture, only 300 years old, as opposed to, say, the Italians with nearly 1,500 years since the early Christian mosaics? Italians revel in visual expression. The French respect it. Moreover, their governments support these efforts. Americans by contrast feel the need to judge, and if they don't like what they see they want to banish the image. Our lives are now bombarded with an overriding abundance of visual images, most of them moving. Clearly, we in America truly need in these times of overwrought hype, shock and sleaze, the rarer, more revealing, more enriching visions of those who deal in images with personal integrity.

STAN BRAKHAGE 1989

I know that the arts are a lonely and hermetic calling, very much like a holy religious order. Those who practice them, all their lives, rather than just as a fluke, say, like those who play at the arts through college, are a part of the tradition that begins with our ancestors who went deep into the mountains—in one case three miles into a mountain—to paint by tallow-light on the walls of the caves they lived in with dyes they had made themselves, these extraordinary cave images. And then, which is in many cases more extraordinary still, they sealed those caves air-tight shut. We know this now. I'm citing the information from Marshak's book *The Roots of Civilization*. We know that this is so because, in some cases, you can actually find the fingerprints in the clay with which these caves are shut. There is other evidence that often only one person made these works deep, deep into the mountain.

Many, many theories abound here. Was this shamanistic activity? Were these paintings only for the gods? At times under tough struggles I've had the paranoid vision that they watched the previous artist in the front of the cave try to put them on the walls and be stoned to death for the effrontery. So they went and buried their work somewhere far away from human eyes. This impulse still moves through people, and you can track all through history that in tough times the art impulse always, always survives. It survives, and it survives in these hermetic ways, shared very closely, carefully and quietly between hermetic makers.

I wanted to raise that image for you here that there not be despair. I know that many people involved both as appreciators and as makers have some despair about these times. For instance, why is it people can't see in this culture this wonder of putting one frame after another and its relationship to putting one word after another? The simplest definition of poetry that I know is that you put one word after another; you're not making a sentence to condemn somebody to your opinion. If you're making a poem, every single word counts, and with filmmakers every 1/48th of a second counts. So at any rate putting these things together, why can't people see? One answer might be that ordinarily, through the hypnotic medium of TV, we present to our children on average six to seven thousand simulated and real violent deaths by the time they are eight or nine. They are always presented within a context which is boxed and taken straight out of the theatre—it is loaded dice. Loaded by the theatre, which is an art form that has been essentially unchanged in human public viewing since the Greeks in the west. That box predisposes everyone to violence in many obvious ways. The whole structure of making a play is to establish certain imbalances which become tensions, to have a violent catharsis and to resolve those tensions. It's axiomatic that in making a theatrical presentation we have a case of loaded dice which suggests annihilation of the human race. And most of us, and I include myself, attend these theatricals fervently in some desperation for what we call escape.

> WHY IS IT PEOPLE CAN'T SEE IN THIS CULTURE THIS WONDER OF PUTTING ONE FRAME AFTER ANOTHER AND ITS RELATIONSHIP TO PUTTING ONE WORD AFTER ANOTHER?

Escape from what? We live a very little time on earth. We know not what is coming or where we have come from. And in that time there is the possibility to fully appreciate while we are here. We haven't until the 1890s had a way to express or share with each other such appreciation of moving visual thinking, which is a level of thinking quite distinct from words and from all other representational symbolic thinking with which painting has been vibrantly involved for centuries. We haven't until 1895, really, had a way to share with each other the inner moving visual thoughts, and it seems to me quite mad, one of the madnesses of our times, to have limited that possibility to making an inexpensive extension of stage drama or moving illustrations for novels of this new medium.

In short, I am not a performer, but a maker of symbolic expressions of the human essence (as I see it) on flat surfaces, marks made with sticks of charred twigs, or with other sticks, with clumps of animal hair tied to one end, dipped in colored liquids....This activity is so primal and so natural, that the idea of getting a medal for doing so is not without irony.

ROBERT MOTHERWELL
1985

WRITE

R S

It's not that literature is an escape from life. *To the contrary, the danger is that life may escape literature.*

JOHN CHEEVER
1979

RICHARD WILBUR

1992

What the Colony offers is an insular experience in the country, a chance to be a landlocked castaway; here one is protected from external distractions, and rewarded with good company in the evenings. Edwin Arlington Robinson, who came here for 23 years, is quoted in Colony literature as saying of this place, "The impulsion to work is in the air," and the visitor senses at once that benign impulsion....

Of course, no man in his seventies can be sure of persisting in his art, especially if he is a lyric poet. When people asked Robert Frost why he wrote poems, he sometimes answered, "To see if I can make them all different." That answer is both evasive and very true; when a poet catches himself not making them all different—repeating not only his themes but his words and devices also—he may feel that it's time for him to stop. Perhaps some writers cease to write because of a change in the audience—the loss of like-minded friends, the disappearance of those mentors and admired elders whom one had set out to please. It may be that age takes away from some artists the ability to be continuously obsessed, day and night, with some developing idea. Archibald MacLeish, in his latter years, said something of the kind to Donald Hall. And then there is the matter of physical vigor. I think that mental energy is not altogether dependent on physical energy; yet I should think that infirmity of sedentariness might rob one's work of strong rhythms and kinetic imagination: When Edmund Spenser speaks of "sea shouldering whales," he is writing with the body, and it may be that writing with the body is something that gets harder to do.

I shall find out about all these things, but for the present I feel—as John Hersey recently said of himself—that "If I were not writing a book I wouldn't know myself."

PRAISING

A WRITER FOR HIS STAMINA may seem like tame stuff—like praising an actor for his enthusiasm or a speaker for the length of his wind. But not to another writer, it doesn't. Writers know what stamina entails: it does not mean treading water. What it does mean is an endless series of rebirths, possibly painful, and always risky. It means forever slashing your way into new parts of the jungle, as opposed to setting up shop in the first clearing one comes to, as the hacks do.

WILFRID SHEED ON
JOHN UPDIKE
1981

JOHN LEONARD on NORMAN MAILER

1973

Flaubert said: "Be orderly and regular in your life, like a bourgeois, so that you may be wild and original in your work." This is probably the one text Norman Mailer hasn't read. He is indiscriminately wild and original, whether he is working or merely living. This causes resentment, especially in the laboratories of the Higher Criticism. We would prefer our literary careers, like the careers of accountants or cultural bureaucrats, to be tidy and correct—even if the world is not. Careers should be tricycles. Like grave children, we would wheel them around the block and then go inside for a bath and a bedtime story by Longfellow. Careers should not be wild horses, derailed locomotives, or moonshots. Walt Whitman does not belong in the nursery.

The excesses of a Mailer are embarrassing. A novelist, an intellectual, should not be a celebrity, a television clown. Mailer the wild-man prophet, this cloud of intuitions and superstitions, this libidinal compost heap, this cyclotron run amok, this nice Jewish boy from Brooklyn wearing his books like strings of grenades—tilting at cancer and plastic and prize-fighting and women's liberation and political conventions and Apollo lift-offs and Marilyn Monroe and secret police and architecture and dread and money and God—that Mailer, making movies and a fool of himself, is unseemly: a stunt-man. And so his highbrow critics come to him armed with a ruler, a compass, a metronome and a pair of scissors. They disapprove of his desire to change history—after all, Henry James didn't want to change history—and of his boyish anxiety to have the rest of us acknowledge that he has indeed altered events. Vainglory: snip: there goes an ear off his pretension. It might be all right to participate in popular culture, but it is not permissible to be popular culture; that's for athletes, movie stars and rock musicians. Snip, snip: no more middle-finger of effrontery. Any writer who appears on the cover of *Time* magazine can't be serious. Snip, snip, snip: ah, now we've cut off the root of the offense. The media and Mailer both agree on his importance; the rest of us are thereby diminished.

Each of us is a performing self. The self discovers itself in its attachments, in its relationships with people and events, relationships between husband and wife, parent and child, imagination and work, energy and duty, power and choice, will and role. What makes the selfhood of a Mailer more interesting than, say, the selfhood of the Watergate 500, is the critical capacity he brings to his relationships, the compulsive empathy, the imagination of disaster....

Mailer is a weird combination of Dickens and D. H. Lawrence, the reporter and the prophet. His past work is full of clues to the future, simply because he paid close attention. Power, in fact, has always been his principal subject; and the two bastard children of power—money and paranoia—in the marketplace, in the bedroom, in the head. He continues to command our attention because there isn't another writer in this country with his 19th-century appetite for social reality in all its forms and deformations—his splendid long-windedness on politics, sports, movies, war, technology, eros—and his willingness to risk himself in the digestion. He actually wants to be a hero. The rest of us, by comparison, are graduate students of nothing more interesting than ourselves, producing little blue-books on how bad we feel about sex or history. One does not make a fool of oneself in the faculty club, and since almost any sort of extravagant activity might cause one to appear foolish, better not to move at all; better to be upholstery....

Mailer wrote about paranoia long before any of us learned that the paranoids are often right. He was obsessed with smells—smell being the key to fear and sex—before our psychologists discovered its importance in the early development of primates.

He worried about plastic before anybody suspected that the credit card mated to the computer would create a class and caste-system, based not on labor, but on the retrieval and exchange of immutable bits of gossip.

He created the New Journalism while all the little boys who run around today crying Tom Wolfe were still on the high school copy desk. He predicted the appearance of the psychopath who cannot be tamed by words, Charles Manson, the self-authenticating gangster, the smarmy satanist. He rummaged in the drawers of biology and genetics for expansive metaphors while most of our custodians of official culture still thought the sciences were as unknowable and as dull as auto repair. He tried drugs, found they burned holes in his brain, and gave them up a generation before our children toyed with self-destruction....

If power and corruption are his principal subject, and stubbornness his intellectual habit, then the secret of his heraldic craft is observation: of himself and anything that moves....

> LITERATURE is a re-run of experience,
>
> its
>
> odd slang-words being the slang of emotions.

I submit that Mailer is one of the few living writers who has made enough observations...to earn the right to guess, which is theory-making and prophecy. His work itself assumes the shape of a deviation hypothesis based on the scatter of social styles. Many of his guesses seem to us to be wrong; many more have been disturbingly accurate. But no dogma attends the guessing; there is no fixed ideological point in the flux of the data, no

MAILER *is incapable of evasions, which is the first qualification for a great writer.* ought to be that obscures what is. Instead, there are lots of mights and maybes. If, he always seems to be saying, this is what human beings are really like, really want to do, then let's devise some scheme that will allow them to be and do it with minimal damage to themselves, to their neighbors and to society....He harps constantly on the theme that instinct, in various deformations appropriate to the powerful and the powerless, will assert itself whether we like it or not. We are cyborgs, compounded as much of our irrational drives as of our capacity to reason and to will. It is dangerously silly to try to wish away the double-helix and the unconscious. The brain itself is divided in conflict....

Mailer admits the instinctual inconvenience, but would cunningly accommodate it. Nothing human can be ultimately suppressed, no matter the critical category or the social system....

Since the turn of the century in Vienna, we should have been aware that language itself disguises the sensations of experience: is only approximate to everything that is chilling or ecstatic. Naming is not knowing, and the torture of words, like the alchemist's torture of metals, doesn't necessarily make for gold. But the writer tries, plundering myth, inflicting puns, using symbols like leeches to bleed the moment of its mystery. Literature is a re-run of experience, its odd slang words being the slang of emotions.

Mailer is incapable of evasions, which is the first qualification for a great writer...when he finds the language inadequate to the modern experience, he seeks to extend the range of language, bringing in animals, swamps, forests, sea-beds, deserts, jungles, smells and the moon: more territory...

he uses his celebrity, not to hustle refrigerators or pogosticks, but to hustle ideas...he is, though a stunt man, deadly serious, our first Russian, our quintessential Spaniard...his naming, his ascriptions of value, his prophecies of what is innate and what is imminent, quite simply enlarge the world we live in, charge it with magic, promise it heroism and treble the number of possibilities for the brave wound and the healing poultice. This is a great chivalry—the stunt-man is our modern version of the medieval knight—and it is unsurprising, morally and politically, that it should risk ridicule. Anybody who tells us that life is much bigger, more exciting, more dangerous, more omen-filled, than we had been allowed to imagine, risks our wish for rude humiliation. The English critic Tony Tanner, in an otherwise tedious essay on Mailer, quotes some marvelously apposite lines from Robert Browning:

> *Ye see lads walk the street*
> *Sixty the minute; what's to note in*
> *that?*
> *Ye see one lad o'erstride a chimney-*
> *stack;*
> *Him you must watch—he's sure to fall,*
> *yet stands!*
> *Our interest's on the dangerous edge*
> *of things.*
> *The honest thief, the tender murderer,*
> *The superstitious atheist...*
> *We watch while these in equilibrium*
> *keep*
> *The giddy line midway: one step*
> *aside,*
> *They're classed and done with.*

Patient ladies and patient gentlemen, I give you our brave stunt man, our Quixote, our genius.

NORMAN MAILER
1973

So the novelist early is out there, I think, like other artists, with that particular necessity, which may become the necessity of us all; that is to deal with life as something that God did not give us as eternal and immutable but rather gave us as something half-worked—half-worked because it was our human destiny to enlarge what we were given, to develop it, either to enlarge or, in developing it, make it so that we've refined it and made it smaller and more perfect, whatever, but that we were here to begin to forge a world which is shifting and treacherous and there always before us in manners different from the way we've seen it the day before.

ELIZABETH HARDWICK on MARY McCARTHY
1984

About Mary McCarthy's writing I suppose the first thing that comes to mind is her mastery of prose composition, of the rhythms and cadences, the sort of classical sonority of her balanced clauses and of course the purity of the diction. These are unusual gifts, but they are instruments in the service of striking ideas argued with passion in the essays and in the fiction expressed by a dramatic imagination.

Along with the prose mastery, the writing reveals a spectacular intelligence and range of learning. Everyone knows that Mary McCarthy is very smart indeed, smart enough from the first of her appearances in print to make some uneasy. I think we might say of her cast of thought that it is both urbane and puritanical, an original and often daunting mixture.

Reading over her fiction, I notice that her characters often have their definition and their dramatic conflict by way of the issues and intellectual fads of the moment, by the manner in which they submit to or fall back from tribal responses. When they speak they may be listened to by the ironical ear of the author; usage and language itself can be a sort of moral x-ray. Turns of speech are not thought to be entirely innocent.

What stays in my mind from my re-reading is the knowledge that the fiction is not dated or in any way narrowed by the political and social details, the follies the decades have wantonly offered to this observing eye. Each story and each novel is as fresh and to the point as when it was written. They are part of a lasting and, I think, very American drama....

Mary McCarthy's essays are discoveries, excavations of a new or old text, and each one is clear, unpredictable and argued with a glittering confidence. She looks at Macbeth once again and discovers in him a bourgeois type, "a murderous Babbitt, let us say." He is the most "modern" of Shakespeare's characters, "the only one you could transpose into contemporary battle dress or a sport shirt and slacks." His soliloquies are not poetry but rhetoric.

In the essay on *Madame Bovary* she wishes to restore a measure of dignity to poor Charles Bovary. "Without Charles, Emma would be the moral void that her fatuous conversations and actions disclose. Charles, in the novelistic sense, is her redeemer. Charles is easy to deceive because his mind is pure. It never enters his head that Emma can be anything but good."

In extracting these movements within the essays I have not done justice to the details of the exposition, the range of interest and knowledge, the exhilaration and imaginative beauty of the conceptions and the renderings.

We might say of her cast of thought that it is both urbane and puritanical, an original and often daunting mixture.

Fearlessness, yes, in the fiction and in the essays. And yet the examination of the work tells me that if Mary McCarthy is a scourge she is a very cheerful one, lighthearted and even optimistic. I do not see in any of her work a trace of despair or alienation but instead rather romantic expectation. She always expects better of persons and of the nation. She seems to believe in love and her heroines are ready to rush out to it again and again. To me this writer from Seattle, New York, Paris and Maine belongs in the line of cranky, idealistic American genius.

MARY McCARTHY
1984

Ladies and gentlemen, in accepting this award I've been driven to review my career, a somewhat saddening business, for I, as person and writer, seem to have had little effect, in the sense of improving the world I came into or even of maintaining a previous standard. Looking around, I can see deterioration in nearly every department of life. The very belief in progress which animated my youth and those poor girls of *The Group* has left us—except, perhaps, in terms of labor saving.

I guess there's a general belief that the Cuisinart is better, even if its products aren't. And the word processor, everyone is sure, is a vast improvement on the old labor-intensive typewriter; if the product is just the same, or worse, the machine will not be faulted....only by me. I like labor-intensive implements and practices, even if I can't persuade anybody to agree with me. In word production, housekeeping, gardening, reading, I actually believe that the amount of labor that goes into a human manufacture determines the success of the enterprise. Whether it's pushing a fruit or vegetable through a sieve, or cranking by hand an ice cream freezer, or going to trouble over a party or a paragraph, the more labor, the better. There's some mystery to it, and there'd be no time here to explain the rationale, if there really is one, behind this persuasion of mine. But I think it has something to do with truth, and with what Michelangelo meant when he spoke of leaving some mark of the tools on the marble rather than have a smooth, polished surface. In late Michelangelo you always have the mark of the tools.

GLENWAY WESCOTT on MARIANNE MOORE 1967

As to her way of working in both prose and verse, sincerity surely is one of her key characteristics. Sometimes it's indistinguishable from spontaneity. Spontaneity takes the lead and brings about inner circumstances in which to be sincere is the honorable, indeed the only reasonable attitude the mind can take. "Spontaneity dies, sincerity swims." Statements about this occur often in her critical and explanatory prose. She speaks about "the helpless sincerity that precipitates a poem." She says that "originality is a by-product of it" and that any writer overwhelmingly honest about pleasing himself is almost sure to please others.

JOHN HERSEY on LILLIAN HELLMAN 1976

Lillian Hellman has long been known as a moral force, almost an institution of conscience for the rest of us—but my view is that her influence, and her help to us, derive rather from something larger: the picture she gives of a life force.

It is the complexity of this organism that stuns and quickens us. Energy, gifts put to work, anger, wit, potent sexuality, generosity, a laugh that can split your eardrums, fire in every action, drama in every anecdote, a ferocious sense of justice, personal loyalty raised to the power of passion, fantastic legs and easily turned ankles, smart clothes, a strong stomach, an affinity with the mothering sea, vanity but scorn of all conceit, love of money and gladness in parting with it, a hidden religious streak but an open hatred of piety, a yearning for compliments but a loathing for flattery, fine cookery, a smashing style in speech and manners, unflagging curiosity, fully liberated female aggressiveness when it is needed, yet a whiff, now and then, of old-fashioned feminine masochism, fear however of nothing but being afraid, prankishness, flirtatious eyes, a libertine spirit, Puritanism, rebelliousness....

Rebelliousness above all. Rebelliousness is an essence of her vitality—that creative sort of dissatisfaction which shouts out, "Life ought to be better than this!" Every great artist is a rebel. The maker's search for new forms—for ways of testing the givens—is in her a fierce rebellion against what has been accepted and acclaimed and taken for granted. And

EVERY GREAT ARTIST IS A REBEL.

a deep, deep rebellious anger against the great cheat of human existence, which is death, feeds her love of life and gives bite to her enjoyment of every minute of it. This rebelliousness, this anger, Lillian Hellman has in unusually great measure, and they are at the heart of the complex vibrancy we feel in her....

In her plays, in her writings out of memory, above all in her juicy, resonant, headlong, passionate self, she gives us glimpses of all the possibilities of life on this mixed-up earth. In return we can only thank her, honor her, and try to live as wholeheartedly as she does.

She and I share a love of the sea. We fish often together. Coming back in around West Chop in the evening light I sometimes see her standing by the starboard coaming looking across the water. All anger is calm in her then. But there is an intensity in her gaze, almost as if she could see things hidden from the rest of us. What is it? Can she see the years in the waves?

COMPO

*what truly matters
in music is that which
can't be imparted except
through itself.*

NED ROREM

ALFRED FRANKENSTEIN on VIRGIL THOMSON
1977

It is fitting that Virgil receive a medal here in New England because Virgil has a New England conscience. He has a great reputation as a wit simply because he tells the truth—and tells it simply. Most of us are such liars by nature and habit that veracity bounces off us as humor; if it struck home, we couldn't stand it....

One day in 1947, when Virgil was preparing the first performance of his opera *The Mother of Us All*, for Columbia University, he played over the score on the piano for Olin Downes and me. It ended with the simplest, clearest, straightest of major triads. Virgil let it die into silence; then he looked up, shook his head, and said, "The only shocker left."

Straightforward statement based on an upbringing in Kansas City is the essence of Thomsonism in Virgil's music. To be sure, it required the paradox of association with Gertrude Stein's far from straightforward text in the earlier opera, *Four Saints in*

HE COMES BACK PERENNIALLY TO THE ONLY SHOCKER LEFT— SIMPLICITY.

Three Acts, to bring Thomsonian clarity to the world's attention; and I have always thought it possible that Virgil had some influence on the far greater clarity and meaningfulness of Miss Stein's second libretto for him, the above-mentioned *The Mother of Us All*. At all events, the latter work, involved as it is with the two most strikingly characteristic of American entertainments—the political convention and the traveling circus—coupled with the heroic joys and sorrows of monomania as exemplified by its protagonist, Susan B. Anthony, is the foremost American opera yet performed. Interestingly, and by no means insignificantly, it has been presented at least a thousand times, infinitely more often than any other American opera, but only once by a professional company, the one in Santa Fe. The rest have all been workshop and college productions.

Thomson has composed in many experimental idioms and understands them all, but he comes back perennially to the only shocker left—simplicity, which he tends to identify with the idioms of 19th-century marches, waltzes, and popular songs; these things, although their style was international, instantly become "American" when they are associated with American dramatic subjects like the passion of Susan B. Anthony. Of course he also works magisterially with folk music, both sacred and secular, which with better reason, we call American.

CHARLES WADSWORTH *on* SAMUEL BARBER

1980

Quite a few composers manage to write simple music which is difficult to understand, but few can write music which is complex and easy to understand. Barber does this. He is unashamedly conservative and romantic and sometimes finds himself out of favor with certain segments of the music community as well as the press. What may happen here is that some listeners may find themselves uncomfortable because they are being moved by his music. This vulnerability might cause some to shy away and underestimate the music, thinking something must be wrong somewhere with music which is so easy to comprehend and enjoy.

NED ROREM on LEONARD BERNSTEIN 1987

We have no sacred monsters anymore, no larger-than-life Stravinskys whose every gesture fires the collective imagination. Even our performing artists are now sold as regular guys, while American saints are fundamentalist hacks snatching expensive haloes from each other.

We have no general practitioners anymore. If in Europe the breed once flourished, from Da Vinci to Cocteau, over here Jacks-of-all-trades have always been suspect. We are specialists. A doctor who treats your foot isn't likely to treat your ear, much less write a play, lest he in turn be treated as superficial. Those blessed with more than one gift are punished for spreading themselves thin.

As sole exception to these assertions we have Leonard Bernstein, the epitome of glamour combined with quality, and thank heaven for him—the heaven of the golden gods of yore.

His triumphs are known to all. No need to reiterate that Bernstein's books and lectures have shaped the way America listens. No need to recall that his mastery of keyboard and podium has defined the notion of American performance. No need to stress that while the scope of his programs spans centuries, it italicizes his homeland, bringing into relief our sense of American craft. Nor is there need to add that as champion of liberal causes he is as scrupulous as to the causes of art.

Now, if he were all this, but had never composed a note, it would, as he has said of others on Passover, have been sufficient. But the notes he has composed are what concern us here today, for the MacDowell Colony, to its very name, symbolizes musical creation even as Bernstein embodies it. And so, for this quarter hour I would like to talk, first, about Bernstein the writer of music, then about Bernstein as he figures in musical society.

He is a composer whose influences on other composers is at once vast and vague. Vast, because in giving Broadway opera a good name—eclectic though he be—he spawned a genre that changed the very skeleton of our musical theater. Vague, because the effect of eclectics on others is by nature as ambiguous as the effect of others on them.

Take my case. Such reputation as I may enjoy seems to lie in songs; and I've always felt that Lenny and I were as different as night and day. Yet last month when I played again his *Jeremiah Symphony*, the first piece of his I ever heard in public, I realized what I may never have wanted to admit—how for decades this heady draught had been infusing my own music. My very first song, on a Chaucer lyric, was modeled on the Hebrew plain in his final movement, and by extension almost every song I've penned has had a taste of his recipe.

What is his recipe?

Start with the rhythm. Bernstein's meters are generally eccentric, even when depicting casualness. Yet despite the off-center basic beat, the assemblage of beats retains a steadiness that inspires listeners to action that involves regular motion, like dancing, picking apples, making love. His tempos, meanwhile, are convincing at any speed, with that potential for infinite variety which distinguishes major from minor artists. His fast music is inherently fast, not slow music played fast, just as his slow music is inherently slow.

His counterpoint is second to none when he chooses, but he doesn't often choose, except sometimes in choral writing. Then he plays different colors against each other, as a great theater man like Verdi does, rather than the same colors at different pitches, as Bach does.

Bernstein's harmony is at once rich and lean. Not only the rainbows conjured from a pure triad, but wildly complex chords are often—they too—expressed in but three voices. His harmony derives from his melody, not the other way around.

Melody, of course, is the sovereign ingredient of music, the one which makes a composer a composer. Without it, nothing else counts. Bernstein's sense of tune is all-embracing, infectious, strange. All-embracing, because it informs every bar of his instrumental catalog, not just the sung airs. Infectious, because once heard it is never forgotten; yet even at the hundredth hearing I, for one, never quite know where it's leading me—which is why it's strange. I do know that Bernstein is the most recent, maybe the last, in the line of great vocal writers that began with Monteverdi, as distinct from the line of more formal writers like Beethoven.

His orchestration, since he's not much given to tricks, stumps the analytic ear with its ingenuousness. As with his tunes, I never know quite how he confects this or that sonority, and the not knowing is, from one composer to another, a high compliment. When, on referring to the score, I discover that his solution for some mystical effect is utterly plain, I wonder why I never thought of it. Still, what truly matters in music is that which can't be imparted except through itself; even the composer isn't always clear about how he makes things tick. Anyone can learn to write a perfect piece, but not how to make that piece breathe and bleed. Bernstein's pieces bleed and breathe. Expressivity is their goal; simplicity their device.

So much for his grammar. What about his language?

People usually speak of derivation as though it were naughty, and not the very soul of composition. All art is clever theft. The act of covering your traces is the act of creation, for that act is you. If you have something to say, that something will gleam through, even though you bend backward to be unoriginal.

He knows that the magic lies not in the communication of sound, but in the sound of communication.

If traces of his beloved Haydn or Mahler exist in Bernstein's scores, they exist only in intent—in the crispness or angst—not in sound. Indeed, I find in him no sound of any musician east of the Rhine. Bernstein's precursors are, rather, Debussy and Copland. Yet the eclectic student's work is instantly recognizable as his own, and those very precursors can be shown to have robbed their past. I have a theory that one can also rob the future. The Debussy theme which Bernstein used for his *Facsimile* was, in fact, a facsimile of Bernstein's simply because the American's use of the theme is more poignant.

As for the Copland connection, the younger man was clearly drawn to the open-air thrift of the older, the unapologetic use of jazz and folk tune, the Parisian transparence of both style and content. Yet Copland somehow seeks to secularize his speech, while Bernstein seeks the reverse. Maybe their very resemblance underlines their basic difference.

What, therefore, is the final effect of Bernstein's ingredients when mixed together—the tunes, lines, pulses, chords, hues, and influences?

All of his music has the theatricality of religious ritual. Not just the Roman Catholicism of his huge *Mass*, which reflects the original multimedia spectacle that for millenniums has been sung, acted, danced, tasted and sniffed, but the High Anglican Waspery of the *Chichester Psalms* and the Audenesque *Age of Anxiety*, the Low Baptist gospel impelling many of his show biz songs and even some of the concert ones, the pristine Hellenism of his Platonic *Serenade*, the medieval cabalism of *Dybbuck*, and the Old Testament tragedy of *Jeremiah Symphony* and *Kaddish*. Even the non-vocal chamber works, like the little *Clarinet Sonata*, seem to have their own scenarios, their exits and entrances and built-in altars at which one prays for a better world.

To define him is, finally, to define any artist. An artist is like everyone else only more so, so Bernstein is like every other artist. Only no other artist is like him.

We first met in early 1943 at his West 52nd Street walk-up. He was already famous, although it would be another eight months before he'd make headlines with his Philharmonic debut. Fame is to some extent a frame of mind, and the young Lenny was every bit as charismatic and self-aware as the star who sits here now.

On his piano, next to Copland's *Piano Sonata*, was a just-finished song called "You've Got To Be Bad To Be Good." I'd have liked using that title for these notes. In fact, yes, experience, including "badness," does aid toward understanding in art, but toward lucid dispersal of art no one knows better than Lenny that you've got to be good to be good. Certainly you've got to be good to be bad—to get away with being bad.

> The most original, up-to-date iconoclasts are all the sum of everything that they have experienced up to that moment, put together, brewed, and recrudesced into what comes out of them.
>
> LEONARD BERNSTEIN, 1987

It's said he's sometimes overbearing, but is that not balanced by his judgment, sense of related values, indeed, by his goodness? Not moral goodness, of course, for art has nothing of morality. He does aim high, but is his aim higher than that of, say, Bruckner, notorious for his modesty? Is Bernstein's unleashed ego really bigger than yours or mine? It's not that he seeks to be the center—he is the center that others seek, for he has that rare knack, which can't be faked or bought, of listening to you alone as though you were the center despite your stammering, or of wanting to convince you alone no less than an audience of thousands.

Still, he soars above the fray, does not appear on talk shows, does not—unlike Stravinsky—lash out at his critics or respond publicly to would-be biographers. He does work hard, and plays hard, but, as befits the sacred monster, he leaves to others the machine of his glory. The more famous some artists grow the more others proclaim, "If only he wouldn't waste himself so!" But waste is not misuse of one's talent, it's lack of use of one's talent—the contrary of Lenny's splendiferous generosity. Still, successful people, if they have brains, don't think of themselves as successful. They know what the public does not know: they know what they've not yet done. Bernstein too wears the crucial badge of all true artists: perpetual self-doubt.

In the intervening smoke-filled insomniac years since 1943, self-doubt notwithstanding, Lenny has brought to life a mountain of first-rate works of his own, and of a hundred colleagues. His premieres of my works have shown that, if as a composer I sometimes become Lenny, as a conductor he turns into me. When performing my music his metabolism is so in tune with my own that he might as well have written the music himself. Other composers here will attest to this; his bloodstream is theirs during the length of their piece.

We live in an unhealthy age where non-pop composers are not even a despised minority. To despise something, that something must exist, whereas our composers are mostly invisible even to the cultured American public who otherwise digs Jackson Pollack or Merce Cunningham or Saul Bellow. Our age is equally unhealthy in that musical taste is determined by non-essential citizens, critics and managers, parasites, who decree that solely music of the past is what counts, for it pays.

Lenny is the only major musical figure in our world who demonstrates that the living creator is the center of his art. Of Bernstein the pacifist, the Socratic rabbi, the un-chic radical, the family man who laughs and reads and loves and dies, it is Bernstein, the composer's interpreter, who is most urgent, for he knows that the composer is his music, just as music is the composer. He alone grasps the ontology of the art. Whatever Bernstein does musically is right, even when it's wrong; the composer is always right, because he is the originator.

"And the performer?" you may well ask at this point. After all, music reviewing has become almost exclusive commentary on the performance of music rather than on the music itself. The performer is that oxymoron: an essential irrelevance. Essential because he displays the music, irrelevant because another performer might do it just as well.

What then of Bernstein, always a composer but sometimes a performer? If he were not a composer he would not be the world's best conductor. Alone among conductors he knows that the essence of music is not what it sounds like, but what the sounds are intended to communicate. Since he too is a composer, he knows that the magic lies not in the communication of sound, but in the sound of communication. He is no more faithful to the score than any performer, but he is faithful always to the composer's intent. A score is but an approximation, while intent is immutable.

Bernstein, on his Omnibus series, was once lauded for taking the magic out of music through his gift of explaining music. But Bernstein does not explain, he reveals. Like the celebrant in his own *Mass*, at the moment of elevation he discloses the sacred elements to all; and we understand that no explanation is possible.

However little I have just said in analysis of both the music and the man, it is still too much. Such analysis cannot be done in words. To think it can is the Critic's Error. Just as critics of words use words, so critics of music use words. The only valid criticism of a piece of music is another piece of music. If you want to know how much I love Lenny, listen to my songs. In discussing any great artist the parts of speech are inadequate. Or as the poet Wallace Stevens says, "Not Ideas about the Thing but the Thing Itself."

And so, precious Lenny, the day is yours, and so is the century. You are what we all would be, the Thing Itself.

MICHAEL STEINBERG on ELLIOTT CARTER

1983

To have your passion and your intelligence spoken to, and to have them spoken to so insistently, as Carter does in his music, that is no small thing. And while I would not presume to say that it's part of his intention, in fact I know that it's not part of his intention, I think one of the wonderful things that happens when one is confronted with music like this is that it can suddenly make you feel very intelligent. You suddenly realize that somebody is speaking to you who thinks that you have a memory, who thinks that you have ears, who thinks that you have powers of attention, who thinks that you do not shrink from passion and drama and excitement. And what greater gift, after all, could we ask from an artist?

> *The field of serious music is wholly based on integrity, and the composer who does not possess it is easily discernible as ungifted, immature, or a fraud.*
>
> JOSEPH POLISI ON DAVID DIAMOND
> 1991

ELLIOTT CARTER

1983

I want to thank everyone concerned with this. And yet I'm not sure that it is really myself that should thank these people. I wonder about that. I hear someone praising me and giving me medals, and it isn't really me that's getting these medals. I feel a little like that old movie with Charlie Chaplin, when the judge started talking to Charlie Chaplin and telling him the awful things he did and Charlie Chaplin looked around to see who it was the judge was talking to.

I have a feeling that somehow there are these shadowy things behind me, these compositions, which are in a way not me, myself; really they deserve the medal and not me. They have this strange life; I'm not sure that I invented them. These strange beings began to come to my mind and gradually somehow insisted on being written in their strange and unusual way, difficult to some people, and profoundly exciting to others. I was just sort of something that wrote them down, because they were telling me they had to be done this way and they were rather trying and sometimes difficult and demanding. And sometimes they did things I had never done before and made me do things that bothered me and upset me and sometimes excited me—and puzzled me, too, sometimes.

EDWARD MacDOWELL MEDALISTS & SPEAKERS

1960 THORNTON WILDER, WRITER
Edward Weeks

1961 AARON COPLAND, COMPOSER
Irving Kolodin

1962 ROBERT FROST, POET
Aaron Copland

1963 ALEXANDER CALDER, VISUAL ARTIST
[in absentia]
Meyer Shapiro

1964 EDMUND WILSON, WRITER
Aaron Copland

1965 EDGAR VARESE, COMPOSER
Milton Babbitt

1966 EDWARD HOPPER, VISUAL ARTIST
[in absentia]
Lloyd Goodrich

1967 MARIANNE MOORE, WRITER
Glenway Wescott

1968 ROGER SESSIONS, COMPOSER
Edward T. Cone

1969 LOUISE NEVELSON, VISUAL ARTIST
John Canaday

1970 EUDORA WELTY, WRITER
       Elizabeth Janeway

1971 WILLIAM SCHUMAN, COMPOSER
       Aaron Copland

1972 GEORGIA O'KEEFFE, VISUAL ARTIST
       [in absentia]
       Lloyd Goodrich (accepted medal)
       Eric Larrabee (spoke)

1973 NORMAN MAILER, WRITER
       John Leonard

1974 WALTER PISTON, COMPOSER
       [in absentia]
       William Schuman (accepted medal)
       Michael Steinberg (spoke)

1974 MARTHA GRAHAM, DANCER
       Special Award
       Agnes de Mille

1975 WILLEM DE KOONING, VISUAL ARTIST
       [in absentia]
       Dore Ashton

1976 LILLIAN HELLMAN, WRITER
       John Hersey

1977 VIRGIL THOMSON, COMPOSER
       Alfred Frankenstein

1978 RICHARD DIEBENKORN, VISUAL ARTIST
John Canaday

1979 JOHN CHEEVER, WRITER
Elizabeth Hardwick

1980 SAMUEL BARBER, COMPOSER
[in absentia]
William Schuman (accepted medal)
Charles Wadsworth (spoke)

1981 JOHN UPDIKE, WRITER
Wilfrid Sheed

1982 ISAMU NOGUCHI, VISUAL ARTIST
William Lieberman

1983 ELLIOTT CARTER, COMPOSER
Michael Steinberg

1984 MARY MCCARTHY, WRITER
Elizabeth Hardwick

1985 ROBERT MOTHERWELL, VISUAL ARTIST
Varujan Boghosian

1986 LEE FRIEDLANDER, PHOTOGRAPHER
John Szarkowski

1987 LEONARD BERNSTEIN, COMPOSER
Ned Rorem

1988   WILLIAM STYRON, WRITER
       George Plimpton

1989   STAN BRAKHAGE, FILMMAKER
       John Hanhardt

1990   LOUISE BOURGEOIS, SCULPTOR
       Robert Storr

1991   DAVID DIAMOND, COMPOSER
       Joseph Polisi

1992   RICHARD WILBUR, POET
       Richard Howard

1993   HARRY CALLAHAN, PHOTOGRAPHER
       Anne Tucker

THE NAME OF ANY ONE OF THESE DEDICATED AND GREATLY GIFTED MEN AND WOMEN COULD NOT FAIL TO INSPIRE ADMIRATION; TAKEN IN AGGREGATE, THE GROUP REPRESENTS THE BRIGHTEST CONSTELLATION OF AMERICAN TALENT THAT COULD BE ASSEMBLED IN THE LATTER HALF OF THIS CENTURY. THE COMBINED POWER OF THEIR CREATION HAS PROVIDED, I SUSPECT, THE INVISIBLE COUNTER-FORCE, THE EQUILIBRIUM, WHICH HAS HELPED KEEP OUR BEDEVILED NATION FROM THE BARBARISM AND DARKNESS— THE POLITICAL VANDALISM—INTO WHICH, SUICIDALLY, IT KEEPS THREATENING TO PLUNGE. THEIR WORK HAS BEEN OF SUPREME VALUE TO THE WORLD, AND TO BE ASKED TO JOIN THEIR COMPANY FLATTERS ME BEYOND MEASURE.

WILLIAM STYRON

1988

This book is printed in the typefaces ITC Galliard and Mantinia. Both were designed by Matthew Carter, and both were based on historical models. Galliard, the text face, was derived from the roman and italic types of the 16th-century French punchcutter Robert Granjon. Mantinia, used for the headings, was influenced by lettering in the ancient Roman style painted and engraved by Andrea Mantegna, artist of the Italian Renaissance.